You Can Get

Answers

To Your

Prayers

Turning Impossible Problems into
Spectacular Answers to Prayer

Eric M. Hill

Published by SunHill Publishers
Atlanta, Georgia 30312

You Can Get Answers to Your Prayers:
Turning Impossible Problems
into Spectacular Answers to Prayer

All rights reserved.
ISBN-13: 978-1534696433
ISBN-10: 1534696431

Unless otherwise noted, Scripture is from the *King James Version,* public domain; or **NKJV**: Scripture taken from the New King James Version®. Copyright © 1982 by Thomas Nelson, Inc. Used by permission. All rights reserved.

You may contact the author at www.ericmhill.com or ericmhillauthor@yahoo.com.

Cover Design by Molly Phipps
https://*WeGotYouCoveredBookDesigns.com*

Let's Stay In Touch!

Join my newsletter at www.ericmhill.com/newsletter. Here's my contact info: ericmhillauthor@yahoo.com or Twitter.com/ericmhillatl.
God bless you!

Other Books by Author

Fiction
Spiritual Warfare

Bones of Fire (The Fire Series, Book 1)
Trial by Fire (The Fire Series, Book 2)
Saints on Fire (The Fire Series, Book 3)

The Spirit of Fear (Demon Strongholds Series, Book 1)
The Spirit of Rejection (Demon Strongholds Series, Book 2)
The Spirit of Ugly (Demon Strongholds Series, Book 3)

Nonfiction

Deliverance from Demons and Diseases
What Preachers Never Tell You About Tithes & Offerings

Table of Contents

Introduction

I am certain that I can help you get spectacular answers to prayer!

Have you ever wondered, What's going on with my prayer? What's taking it so long to be answered? Or worse, Why wasn't it answered? Confession time. I certainly have. And after forty years in ministry, I can tell you that many wonderful Christians are asking these same questions. They read promises in the Bible such as, "Ask, and it shall be given you; seek, and you shall find; knock, and it shall be opened to you. For everyone who asks, receives, and he who seeks, finds, and to him who knocks it will be opened" (Matthew 7:7, 8).

The first time a Christian reads a promise like this, she's ecstatic. "Wow! Let's pray!" Yet, given time and a series of disappointing results in prayer, she's reduced to something sad. She still loves God and trusts that when she dies, she will go to heaven. But she finds it difficult, if not impossible, to believe that she can experience many of the Bible's promises now.

At this point, some Christians grow bitter and cold and fall away from the faith. Others don't go down such a drastic road. Instead, they adjust their Christian belief system downward to expect little in the way of regular, unmistakable, and definitely not, spectacular answers to prayer.

My desire with this short book is to use biblical truth and personal examples of spectacular answers to prayer to show you exactly how to get your own regular, and often spectacular, answers to prayer. No theory. No fluff. Each chapter ends with a list of lessons that we'll use together to design prayer templates you can use to help you get regular and often spectacular answers.

Specifically, I am going to explain to you how to pray about problems and situations that haven't yet yielded to your prayer efforts. In Christian terminology, this refers to *strongholds*. Strongholds are exactly what the name denotes. They are situations or problems that have an above average strong hold. Every effort you've taken against the stronghold up to this point may have been good, but not good enough.

Why is this? And how do you turn a stronghold into a spectacular answer to prayer? By God's grace and mercy, that's what I'm going to share with you in the following pages—biblical truth and actionable methods.

Don't worry. The information I give you will also help with situations that may not technically be a stronghold, but nonetheless are serious. For the record, everything I share with you is under the assumption that you love and serve the Lord Jesus Christ.

This doesn't mean that you don't make mistakes, that you don't struggle with sin, or that there aren't things about your life that grieve your own spirit. It simply means that you have and presently do acknowledge Jesus Christ as Lord of your life and that you live a life of true repentance before the Lord. And if you haven't yet reached this point, perhaps by the time you finish this little book, you will have done so. Don't be discouraged. As the Scripture says, "For God is able to make him [you] stand" (Romans 14:4).

Come on. Let's demolish your strongholds and get spectacular answers to prayer!

Chapter One
Spectacular Answers to Prayer Are Real

*"Behold, I am the Lord, the God of
all flesh. Is there anything too hard
for Me?"*

Jeremiah 32:27

No, I'm not being mean and rubbing salt in the wound of unanswered prayer. On the contrary, I'm assuming that you may have suffered a prayer defeat here and there that has left you needing someone to remind you that answered prayer is real. Of course, there are stories galore in the Bible of spectacular answers to prayer, but guess what? We're not in the Bible! So what you need to be reminded of is that although you do not yet receive regular, spectacular answers to your prayers, many other people do.

But how does that help me? you may ask. It helps because if no one is getting their prayers answered, there may be no rational reason for you to expect to get yours answered. However, if others are getting their prayers answered, since we know God is no respecter of persons, there is no reason why you can't make some adjustments and start getting your prayers answered. So let's start with a real life example of someone receiving a spectacular answer to prayer—that someone being me and my wife.

The Worse Time to Sell a House…
Unless You Know How to Pray

Shortly before the housing bubble collapsed in 2006, I felt that God was leading us to move from the suburbs into the city so that our home could be centrally located in the Atlanta metropolitan area. For ministry purposes, it would be ideal. No problem, right? Sell the house and purchase another one. Millions of people do it all the time, and without prayer!

Well, there was a problem. Actually, more than one.

First, no one in our subdivision could sell their home. The realtor said it took an average of eight months to sell. That wasn't going to work for us. Oh, I didn't tell you? I had done something that was foolish from a natural, business perspective. I had put a contract on another home!

People do that, too, all the time. However, we were not at a place financially where we could pay two mortgages without hurting. *The reason I did something like this was because I was convinced God was leading me.* Without getting ahead of myself, I'll briefly state that is one of the secrets to getting spectacular answers to prayer.

Hearing God.

Had I not been thoroughly convinced that God was in my decision, there is absolutely no way I would have gone out on a limb like that!

Second, I put the house on the market in December or January. My realtor said the rule was that homes sell badly in the winter. I had chosen the worst possible time to sell.

Third, our neighbors on the immediate left and right of us had put their homes up for sell months before we did. We watched them finally remove the *For Sale* signs in defeat.

So, what happened? Glad you asked. We sold the home in two months for the full asking price. My neighbors were shocked. Great story, but the following is the spectacular part.

The part that's going to help you get your own spectacular answers.

"Honey, that doesn't apply to us."

Early after deciding to sell our home, *and* after my wife and I had heard the dismal forecast from our realtor about the eight-month average selling time, *and* the fact that it was a buyer's market, *and* the fact that if we were serious about selling, we'd have to drastically drop the price, I said something that you're going to be able to say once you finish this book. I said, "Honey, I understand all of that, but those limitations don't apply to us."

Arrogant? Presumptuous? Denial? Nope, nope, and nope.

The reason those limitations didn't apply to us was because God had taught me how to pray for spectacular answers during the first year after I received salvation. I've been using these principles and practices ever since. Briefly, here is what happened with the house ordeal.

I told my wife that I'd change the situation through prayer. Now since each day that we didn't have our home sold meant we were one day closer to taking on a second mortgage, this added an element that is often there in strongholds. This was the element of a time deadline.

Deadlines can be soft or hard. A soft deadline is one where the world doesn't end when the deadline comes. However, things do get pretty bad. A hard deadline is where, barring a Lazarus type miracle from God, your situation explodes in your face with finality.

My deadline, though serious, was soft. It was soft because if the house didn't sell, I could've used my savings to pay the second mortgage. Once the savings were gone, however, the deadline would've turned hard because now I would be facing the loss of my home.

We had a lock box on our door so realtors (and hopefully their clients!) could access the home when we were away. There was that initial rush of realtors to look at the home. They left their cards in a bowl. Lots of cards, no buyers.

Each day after work, I'd take that soft deadline down to the basement and present it to God in prayer. My first goal was not to allow the soft deadline to turn hard. The prospect of depleting our savings and finally losing our home was ample motivation to keep me praying as I waited for the spectacular to happen. We'll call this motivation *a sense of urgency*. This will come up later.

I've already told you that the prayer was spectacularly answered. So, no mystery there. But what did I do in that basement that caused God to sell our house and leave other would-be home-sellers on our left and right scratching their heads and asking us how we did it?

I like to walk as I pray. I've found it's quite difficult to fall asleep in prayer if I'm walking. It also helps me to focus. So, there I am in the basement walking around with a bowl of realtor cards lifted over my head.

Sometimes I was down there for up to a couple of hours. I'd worship my Father and tell Him how much I loved Him. I'd remind myself of all the good things He had already done for me and thank Him for it. I'd talk to Him about the stories in the Bible I'd read about Him performing great miracles for people who had no other hope but Him.

I'd remind Him that I had signed the other contract only because I was convinced He wanted me to do it. I told Him that although I had signed the contract because by faith I was trying to follow His leading, I could have been mistaken (although I didn't think I was). I asked Him to have mercy on me if I had indeed made a mistake.

I shared with Him what would happen if He didn't help. told Him that I knew we wouldn't be helped, and He wouldn't receive glory if my bank account was depleted and we lost our home. I'd also point and jab my finger at the floor or at the ceiling and shout at the dark powers of Satan and declare that God was my Father and that He was listening to my prayers. I quoted or read Scriptures out loud to myself, to the devil, and to God.

There are Scriptures in the Gospels where Jesus told His disciples that they could release unfathomable power in their behalf if they spoke to problems in His name and had faith that the problems would obey them (Matthew 21:18-22). Crazy stuff, I know! But whoever said Jesus was ordinary? And who started and spread the lie that His followers were to be ordinary? I think we know who this is.

So, in obedience to words in the Bible that seem utterly ridiculous, I obeyed. I'd point and jab my finger figuratively at the problem of a house that, according to the expert, couldn't sell unless I drastically dropped the price. I'd say things like this:

> *I know what my realtor says. I know what the market says. I know that no one in this subdivision can sell their home unless they practically give it away. I know that my neighbors on both sides of us have put For Sale signs out and have had to pluck them up again in frustration.*

> *But you listen to me, mountain! I am a son of God, a child of the Most High God. You don't dictate my limitations; He does. My Father gives life to the dead. He brought Lazarus back after he was dead four days. He made water come out of a rock for Moses. He fed the prophet Elijah in famine*

and drought by commanding a bird to deliver food to him twice a day.

There is nothing my great God can't do. His word tells me that you must obey my command if I speak to you in faith. Well, listen up, oh mountain! Mountains were made to be moved. I command you in Jesus's mighty name to move. House, I command you to sell!

Now, precious son or daughter of God, in the presence of God and knowing that I will have to give a public accounting of my words on that great day of judgment, I tell you without the slightest embellishment, this is what I said next (the spectacular part!):

I see that the weather has been bad and no one has been coming by to look at the home. I command people to come look at our home. Furthermore, oh mountain, I see you sitting there and looking at me. I hear your mocking laughter. You say, "I'm a mountain, and you're just a puny little man. You can't make me move!" Well, this is my response! Lord God, I thank You right now in the face of this great mountain. I declare that this mighty mountain is being moved, and in a little while I will see with my natural eyes that which has already happened, as far as I'm concerned.

Father, I'm only selling one house. I know that somewhere in this world there is a person who would be blessed by purchasing our home. And, Lord, I know there's someone out there willing to pay full price for it. I ask You to find and direct this person here. [Check out my next words!] *Lord, it doesn't matter if they're from out of town. It doesn't matter if they've already signed a contract with someone else. You are able to cause this person to fall in love with our home. You're able to work this situation out so that no one is hurt financially. I ask You to bring that person to us.*

I continued to pray this way. One day soon thereafter, my wife was sleeping and heard a loud voice shout, "Exit!" She jumped up wondering what it meant. For the next several days, whenever she went to an enclosed area, she searched out the exit and made sure she was ready to make her exit. Why else would the Lord give her such a dream? (From time to time we receive dreams from the Lord and figured this was another.)

Well, there was another reason the Lord shouted, "Exit!" One day I came home from work and looked in the bowl for any new realtor cards. There was only one. Guess what was on the card. Come on, you can do it. Yep, Exit Realty. Guess who sold our home. Right again. Exit Realty. What a coincidence, you say. I say it was our loving Father letting us know He answers prayer.

Remember that part of my prayer to God where I specifically said, "Lord, it doesn't matter if they're from out of town. It doesn't matter if they've already signed a contract with someone else. You are able to cause this person to fall in love with our home. You're able to work this situation out so that no one is hurt financially. I ask You to bring that person to us"?

The lady who purchased our home was from New York. She was in town for only one weekend and had to purchase a home that weekend. She had already placed a contract on a home. Yet, we found out from her realtor that when she walked into our home, she said, "I feel the peace of God here. This is it. It's the house."

And the rest is history.

Now don't jump on me because I included in my prayer for God to include in His search people who had already signed a contract. It was up to Him to find a buyer and seller who wouldn't be hurt if He used them to answer my prayer.

Prominent Elements of My Prayer

We will explain these elements in detail later. But I want to list them now so you'll have a clearer understanding as we proceed. God isn't a system to be manipulated or a formula to plug into a prayer request. He's Almighty God. By the very definition of being *God*, no one can make Him do anything.

So, let's be clear that I am not listing how I made or manipulated our Creator and Lord and Savior and Judge to do *my* bidding. I am listing how He helped me do *His* bidding. Quite a difference!

Element One. I recognized the problem as the mountain it was, but I compared the mountain to God's ability to move it.

Element Two. I believed I had been in the will of God when I created part of this scenario by signing the second house contract. (Think David and Goliath. Where does the Bible say God told him to challenge Goliath? Wasn't it, shall we say, from a natural perspective...*foolish?*)

Element Three. I committed myself to change the situation through prayer.

Element Four. I had a sense of urgency to change the situation.

Element Five. I quoted the word of God out loud to myself, to Satan, and to God.

Element Six. I spoke to the mountain in faith just as Jesus said we should.

Element Seven. I prayed with great fervency and many tears.

Element Eight. I talked to God in great detail about the threat of the problem and the great blessing in having it removed.

Element Nine. I praised and worshipped God before, during, and after my prayers.

Element Ten. I asked God for something ridiculous and expected a spectacular answer.

Element Eleven. I boldly approached God's throne for mercy to help in my time of need.

Element Twelve. I believed that despite my imperfections that our great God and Father wanted to help me.

See How Easy It Is?

I say the above in jest. Trust me. Although it's not complicated, it's often not obvious how you should pray. If it were, there'd be no need for books like this one. Nonetheless, you're on your way to getting regular and spectacular answers to prayer. But you need to know there is a single ingredient of getting spectacular answers to prayer that often—not always, hallelujah!—challenges the most seasoned Christians. Here it is in all of its formidable simplicity.

It is acting upon the mountain with
biblical prayer principles and
waiting patiently and expectantly

on God for the answer while and
after you pray.

We'll take a brief look at a few people who were facing mountains and who I had the privilege of teaching these prayer principles. Since they were members of our church, I was blessed to be able to personally see them get spectacular answers to their prayers.

Afterwards, we'll systematically examine in detail what's all involved in getting these kinds of prayer answers. We'll end each chapter with *Lessons Learned* to help you easily see the main points. We'll also go through some practical exercises and ways to get your own prayers answered. You'll be pleasantly surprised to find that not all spectacular answers to prayer take a long time to come. Some come shockingly fast!

Prayer Hit List Action Plan

Imagine you've been invited by God into His throne room. You sit across from Him. He smiles at you and pushes a piece of paper and pen across to you. He asks you to write down a prayer wish list. Do it. Review the list as you read this book. Later, you may find yourself adding things and removing others.

Chapter Two
When the Mountain Says No, Move the Mountain through Prayer

Now in the morning, as He returned to the city, He was hungry. And seeing a fig tree by the road, He came to it and found nothing on it but leaves, And said to it, "Let no fruit grow on you ever again." Immediately the fig tree withered away.
And when the disciples saw it, they marveled, saying, "How did the fig tree wither away so soon? So Jesus answered and said to them, "Assuredly, I say to you, If you have faith and do not doubt, you will not only do what was done to the fig tree, But also if you say to this mountain, 'Be removed and be cast into the sea,' It will be done. And whatever things you ask in prayer, believing, You shall receive."

(Matthew 21:18-22)

Promises like the one above seem so out of reach for us ordinary Christians that we either skip over them or explain them away. Better to put the promise in the basement than to have to live under its mocking voice.

Great news! We're unlocking the basement door and letting this great promise out. Look what happened to personal friends of mine once they put the contents of this book into action.

Your Dental School Application is Denied...
Unless You Know How to Pray

John is a wonderful Christian. He's smart, too. He graduated with a double major from Georgia Institute of Technology. But sometimes no matter how smart you are, it's not enough. You see, his passion was to become a dentist and to periodically provide free dental services as a medical missionary. Standing directly in the path of this God-given dream was a mountain. The name of this mountain was *Dental School Rejection.*

He applied to many schools and was denied. His Dental Admission Test scores were decent. They were within the range of others who had been accepted. He was at a complete loss as to why he was being rejected. Of course, many people are not accepted into dental school. It's a normal part of life. The question, however, was as a son of God was he subject to this limitation?

John came up for prayer about this matter one evening at our church. I shared with him that he wasn't subject to this limitation because God could overrule everyone who was denying him. I shared with him how I had gone directly to God many times when the mountain had said no and ultimately God had overruled the mountain. I told John to cry out to God and to thank Him for removing the mountain even before there was any natural evidence that it had been removed.

I then instructed him to go right back to those dental schools that had rejected him. I told him that because of his prayers, God could do one or more of several things to get him into dental school. He could change the hearts of those who had denied him. He could replace those people with others who would accept him. He could create a new program that would provide him a slot. Or He could do that God thing He does so often and baffle our minds with His creativity and power.

We went over Scriptures like Jeremiah 33:3, "Call to Me, and I will answer you, and show you great and mighty things, which you do not know." *Which you do not know.* Think God opening the Red Sea to save the Hebrews from the Egyptian army (Exodus 14). Think Jesus multiplying a few fishes and loaves of bread to save thousands (Matthew 15:32-38).

There is no way you or I would've imagined either of those moves by God. His influence, power, and creativity are infinitely beyond our ability to figure out. That's why we shouldn't spend too much time considering how difficult it would be for God to answer our prayers. Our part is to ask; His part is to answer.

Oh, and I guess you've figured out John's story. The school *coincidentally* started a new program that allowed him to be accepted. He is now a dentist!

Oh, how I love those coincidences!

You're Stuck at This Financial Level…
Unless You Know How to Pray

Kenny and Abbey are wonderful Christians. They'd been dating for quite a while. Marriage was definitely an item of interest for them both. However, Kenney's financial history and status, and his career path had built-in challenges that Abbey felt should best be changed prior to them getting married.

The mountain was that there was absolutely nothing in Kenny's past or anticipated future to give them a realistic reason to think the situation would change for their good. So, Abbey listened to my teachings about pressing in to God in prayer. She discussed this with Kenny, and they agreed to change the situation through prayer. You know what's coming now, don't you? Yep, another coincidence.

It took about two or three months of them crying out to God and using the twelve elements of prayer listed in chapter one. Wouldn't you know it? A friend of Kenny learned through a friend that there was a great job coming open at one of the major airlines. Kenny's friend lobbied heavily to get his friend to consider Kenny.

In a little while Kenny was hired. Today he walks around with a permanent smile on his face, happy with his beautiful bride, Abbey, and gushing about his high salary and great benefits. Think of it. Decades of financial ruin and dead-end jobs spectacularly turned around through a few months of intelligent, fervent prayer.

In the following chapters, we'll dissect the anatomy of prayers that are spectacularly answered. You're going to learn exactly how to imitate others who receive great answers to prayer.

You're next in line to receive your own, precious child of God!

Lessons Learned

Lesson One. Other Christians are getting spectacular answers to prayer and so can I!

Lesson Two. No doesn't have to remain no if I know how to pray!

Practical Exercise

1. Look at your prayer list. After reading about God so dramatically answering other people's prayers, do you need to add anything to your list?

2. Use your imagination to think of "coincidences" that could bring your prayers closer to becoming reality. Write the coincidences down. God has unlimited creativity; so He doesn't need the coincidences you write down. But keep your eyes and ears open. Don't be surprised if He uses a couple of them just to let you see He's with you.

Chapter Three

Recognize the Problem As the Mountain It Is, But Compare It to God's Ability to Move It

"But He [Jesus] said, 'The things
which are impossible with men
are possible with God."

Luke 18:27

The Scripture above shows that Jesus recognizes the impossibilities of men. If you are going to get regular and spectacular answers to prayer, you must be based in reality. Ignoring a problem or pretending it isn't as big or as serious as it is, isn't faith. It's foolishness.

A few decades ago, the word of faith movement gained popularity in the church, mainly the portion that considers itself charismatic. After a few years of retrospect, it can be safely said that like other genuine moves of God (e.g., the Reformation; see Persecutions of the Reformation on the internet), much good and much bad resulted.

The good was that the power of faith in God and His word were taught in detail with great consistency. Millions of people found that the God of the Bible hadn't changed one bit. He still answered prayer, and He still worked miracles. Subsequently, the Holy Spirit responded to this new atmosphere of faith in marvelous power—He is still responding!

2 Chronicles 16:9 was realized: "For the eyes of the Lord run to and fro throughout the whole earth to show Himself strong on behalf of those whose heart is loyal to Him..." Think

of it. God actively searches for people to bless. The word of faith folks crammed this truth into our faces. I for one am grateful.

Nonetheless, the bad that came from this movement was very bad. Ambitious and enterprising preachers polluted the movement with their greed, covetousness, dishonesty, and astounding biblical ignorance. The point that fits in with our march toward spectacular answers to prayer is *ignorance*.

One of the extreme doctrines that came from this movement encourages people directly or indirectly not to speak anything negative. Well, I'm all for not being a negative person, but this doctrine goes lightyears beyond addressing a negative disposition. It actually condemns an honest assessment of the mountain. It's considered doubt, fear, or unbelief to acknowledge that the situation is horrible and getting more horrible by the moment.

Listen to me...please! No amount of ignoring a cancer will stop it from growing or spreading. No amount of ignoring bills will keep your utilities from being cut off or you from being put out on the street.

I have a friend, an absolutely incredible woman of God who is so far ahead of me in some Christian graces that I can't even see her in the horizon. Nonetheless, it's hard to talk to her when she's facing a mountain. She's so afraid of undoing her faith by an errant word that it's hard to get a straight answer from her about what's going on in her life.

It's like, "Mary, I see you standing there in the rain. Do you need a ride?"

"Glory to God, all my needs are met," she answers.

The disconnect here is I'm asking her about her practical need and she's responding by telling me what spiritual truth she believes. So, I smile and drive off. Guess what? She just missed the ride God sent her. Do not think this is a

hypothetical extreme. Unfortunately, it's all too familiar. Bu
not in the next story.

Admitting That the Mountain is a Mountain Won't Damage Your Faith If You Compare the Mountain to God's Power

Part One
*"Then some came and told
Jehoshaphat, saying,
'A great multitude is coming
against you...And Jehoshaphat
feared, and set himself to seek the
Lord, and proclaimed a fast...
So Judah gathered together to ask
help from the Lord...they [the
nation] came to seek the Lord.*

Part Two
*Then Jehoshaphat stood in the
assembly...and said, 'O Lord God of
our fathers, are You not God in
heaven, and do You not rule over
all the kingdoms of the nations,
and in Your hand is there not
power and might, so that none is
able to withstand You? O our God,
will You not judge them?
For we have no power against this
great multitude that is coming
against us; nor do we know what
to do, but our eyes are upon You."*

2 Chronicles 20:12

This story shows how to properly look at a mountain. This is crucial because your perspective of the mountain will determine your prayer and your behavior after prayer. Often post-prayer behavior slows down, complicates, or totally stops the answer. So, it's absolutely critical that we understand this lesson.

Part one of the story shows the mountain in all its power: Judah was vastly outnumbered by the huge armies that were coming against it. The king could've said, "Bless God, don't worry about the bad report. We don't want to glorify the devil by talking about what he's doing. Doesn't the 91st Psalm say, 'A thousand shall fall at our side, and ten thousand at our right hand; but it shall not come near us'?"

Notice in part one that the king does something that ordinarily is considered negative in the Christian context.

And Jehoshaphat feared.

Now how many times have we been blasted by faith preachers for having fear? Uh, a lot! I'll go a reverent step farther. How many times did Jesus rebuke the disciples for their fear? A lot. So, isn't fear bad? Isn't it the automatic kiss of death for getting prayers answered?

I think not. I think faith preachers have missed it terribly here. In baseball parlance, they've hit the ball and run directly to third base. And as far as Jesus's admonitions against fear are concerned, we've simply struck out. We didn't understand the context of His words.

Fear certainly *can* derail prayer answers if we let it, but this isn't inevitable. Jehoshaphat feared and received a spectacular answer to prayer. How can you imitate Jehoshaphat and get your prayers answered even though you feel fear? Start by understanding two things.

First, the absence or presence of fear doesn't mean you are either in or out of faith. It is simply an involuntary emotion that the brain produces when it perceives a dangerous threat. You don't turn off fear by declaring it's gone, pretending it's gone, or quoting a Scripture. And since you don't need to get rid of fear to get your prayers answered, I suggest you spend very little time getting rid of fear.

Second, Jesus's commands to "fear not" doesn't mean don't *feel* fear; it means don't *obey* fear. Isn't He the one who said, "But I will show you whom you should fear: Fear Him who, after He has killed, has power to cast into hell" (Luke 12:5). Was the object of the Lord's words simply to get us to *feel* an emotion? Was it not to get us to *obey*?

Absolutely. God knows that behavior follows what we fear. For instance, when He says in Revelation 21:8 that the fearful will suffer eternal doom, was He saying those who *feel* fear are doomed? No. In this context, and indeed whenever the Lord rebukes fear (you can check this by examining such references in the Gospels), He is talking about allowing fear to keep us from obeying Him.

Back to Jehoshaphat. Can you imagine being told you're being surrounded by Isis, and then trying not to have fear? Are—you—kidding—me? Jehoshaphat did what I encourage you to do. He honestly and realistically looked at the threat…and subsequently felt fear. But! But! But! He didn't stay focused on the fear. And I couldn't hardly wait to say this: Instead of letting his fear stop his answer to prayer, he used the power of fear to increase a sense of urgency and to push him into the presence of God.

A sense of urgency in prayer is often needed to get certain prayers answered. And getting into the presence of God is *always* needed. This is why I am laboring on this point of Jehoshaphat's fear. If you don't admit how big and dangerous the threat is, you may not find the focus and intensity you need to hold on in prayer until its power is broken and the prayer is answered.

Follow Jehoshaphat's example. Be honest about what you're facing, and if this admission causes a so-called negative emotion, whether it's fear, grief, worry, or whatever, let that thing drive you to your knees. Trust me. If you do this, you won't have to try to spend more time in prayer. You won't have to try to be more focused in prayer. You won't have to try to be more fervent in prayer. The mountain will make sure you have all of these things in abundance!

Jehoshaphat Took His Mountain To God, And So Can You!

Part two of Jehoshaphat's prayer is the good part. He did two things that are part of successful prayer results, especially spectacular results. First, he acknowledged *and spoke out loud* the general greatness of God. That's always good, but he went a step farther. Second, he transitioned from speaking in general terms of God's mighty power to specifically asking God to use His mighty power in the nation's behalf.

Remember this: It's not enough to acknowledge that God is great and powerful. At some point, you have to transition to asking God to use that mighty power and influence for your specific situation.

Let these words of Jehoshaphat roll around in your heart. Say them out loud a few times. "For we have no power against this great multitude that is coming against us; nor do we know what to do, but our eyes are upon You."

Jehoshaphat didn't minimize the threat, did he? He felt overwhelmed, didn't he? He had fear, didn't he? Yep, yep, and yep. Didn't stop him one bit! Why? For the same reasons you won't be stopped. He acknowledged this horrible threat. It produced fear. He let the fear drive him to prayer. In the presence of fear, while praying, he reminded himself of God's power and spoke this out loud. He then admitted that he didn't know what to do. Finally, he said out loud, "But my eyes are on You."

You won't be stopped because your eyes are on God!

Lessons Learned

Lesson One. It is not a lack of faith to honestly assess my need, the presence of a mountain, or the power and danger of the threat, if there is one.

Lesson Two. The presence of fear before or during prayer is not an automatic faith or prayer killer. I should use fear and other negative emotions generated by the mountain to drive me to my knees. I should continue this process until I know in my heart or I see with my eyes that the prayer is answered.

Lesson Three. I must remember that the things that are impossible for people are possible for God. He has unlimited power, influence, and creativity. I should believe God well beyond my ability to figure out how He will answer my prayers.

Lesson Four. As I take my issue to God, I should orally speak of His power. And at some point, I must transition to asking God to use that mighty power and influence for my specific situation.

Practical Exercise

1. Do you have a mountain in your life? Is so, write it down.

2. Think of what happens if that prayer were to never be answered. Scary thought? Good.

3. Be honest with God about the bigness of the mountain. Tell Him with your mouth how big the mountain is. *Don't be afraid. This isn't unbelief; it's actually faith!*

4. Now imitate Jehoshaphat. Say, "Lord, I don't know what to do, but my eyes are upon You!" Say this out loud several times. Feel the spirit of faith come over you. Now with your eyes closed and hands raised, let the Holy Spirit feed faith thoughts to your mind about God's ability to fix this situation. You don't have to know *how*, just that He is able.

Chapter Four

It Is Critical to Know You Are Asking According to God's Will When You Pray

"Now this is the confidence that we have in Him, that if we ask anything according to His will, He hears us. And if we know that He hears us, whatever we ask, we know that we have the petitions that we have asked of Him."

1 John 5:14, 15

I heard the sigh of frustration. That's one of the problems isn't it? Often we don't know the will of God; so how can we pray in confidence, especially if the answer is delayed? Good news! God didn't give you the promises above to tease or frustrate you. He wants your prayers answered.

How to Pray According to the Will of God

Let's begin with what's not mysterious. There are innumerable Scriptures which tell us what to do and not do. For instance, 1 Thessalonians 5:18 says, "In everything [in, not *for*] give thanks; for this is the will of God in Christ Jesus for you."

You don't have to search for Scriptures like these; they're everywhere. So are the others which don't have "this is the will of God" in them, but nonetheless are as clear and directive as those that do. So, it is entirely possible that the answer you're searching for in prayer has already been revealed in the Bible. You may be able to cut down your prayer time considerably (at least for the object you're presently praying) by aggressively searching the Scriptures. I suggest starting by carefully reading through Proverbs.

However, you won't find a Scripture that says, "Marry Blake; he'll make a great husband and father, and you'll never regret your decision." Sure, you will find a ton of Scriptures about relationships and marriage and commitment and so forth, but none of them will mention Blake. This is where things start feeling like a dangerous coin toss. Thank God, there's a better way!

Is Your Prayer Paralyzed Because You Don't Know What God Wants?

Christians are often paralyzed in place, afraid to go left or right, for fear of missing God. Now waiting on God before big decisions is good, but when taken to an extreme, it works against our prayers. I've talked to Christians who purported to be so spiritual that literally everything about them was "Spirit led." Sounds awesome; actually awful.

This one real example represents what I'm speaking of. A woman told me she was so led of the Spirit that she didn't even dress herself until she was sure of the exact clothing God wanted her to wear. To me this is cringe worthy because my understanding of the Scriptures leads me to believe God gets glory from our growth in Him, and from the decisions that arise from that growth.

God gets no glory from a daughter of God sitting on the side of the bed waiting for Him to tell her which socks and bra to wear. This may appear silly and a waste of space in a book this size; it's not. It's directly related to praying in the will of God.

Imagine the prayer life of a person who thinks like this. If she can complicate something as simple as what clothes to wear, prayer must be an exceeding complicated task for her. I know she's an extreme case. And in all honesty, I've only dealt with a few people who go this far. Yet many Christians who would never ride the bus as far as this lady does, are in fact on her bus. And in my over forty years of serving Christ, I've talked to bunches of Christians like this.

To illustrate, I read an article about mental illness. It discussed the different levels of mental illness. For the sake of simplicity, let's say on a scale of one to ten, ten qualifies as the level where a person's life is functionally disrupted and perhaps noticeable to others. The article went on to say that tens of millions of people are at levels that don't reach the severity of ten, but are at high enough levels that they possess extremes in their emotions, judgment, and perspective. Functionally normal, but compromised.

Similarly, many otherwise outstanding Christians who don't wait for God to tell them what clothes to wear each day do possess a milder version of this paralysis. They go about their lives routinely making hundreds of decisions, some of them quite important, based upon common sense, academic or specialized knowledge, Scriptural encouragement or prohibitions, growth in Christ and experience with God, among other things.

Nonetheless, often when it comes to seeking God for specific things in prayer that aren't clearly spelled out in Scripture, they wipe the board clean and promptly forget everything they've been doing to this point.

They default to "I don't know how to pray in this situation because I don't know what God wants here." And since they don't know *exactly* what God wants, they can't pray with the confidence spoken of in our Scriptures, 1 John 5:14, 15.

I understand. Trust me. There are some situations that are so complicated and time critical and potentially far reaching in their effects that we don't want to flip a spiritual coin and hope for the best. So, I'm not blasting you for hesitating to thump the coin into the air. What I want you to see is you don't have to call heads or tails. God has a better way. And it's one hundred percent His will—always!

What Did Paul Do When He Didn't Know Exactly What God Wanted?

I don't believe we need *to know* exactly what God wants for us *to do* exactly what He wants. The apostle Paul wrote two-thirds of the New Testament and was, according to the Holy Spirit, the greatest of the apostles. He certainly knew what we call the great commission: "Go into all the world and preach the gospel to every creature" (Mark 16:15).

Yet we see him going about his missionary journeys in Acts 16:6-10 making what we might call mistakes or presumptuous decisions in his attempt to obey God. He tried to go into Asia (not our geographical Asia) and "they were forbidden by the Holy Spirit to preach the gospel in Asia." So they went to a place called Mysia and "tried to go into Bithynia, but the Holy Spirit did not permit them."

What were the others thinking? "Wow, I'm trusting this guy with my life, and he has no idea what he's doing. Why, he's just flipping a coin!" Just when the board was about to call a secret meeting to discuss Paul's inability to hear from God, Paul had a vision directing them to go to Macedonia.

How does this relate to you praying in confidence when you don't know the *exact* will of God? Look at Paul. If we conclude that him knowing the exact will of God meant knowing which direction and destination to go, then he clearly didn't know. Yet in the end, he arrived *exactly* where God wanted him. What happened for him can and will happen for you.

Paul didn't know the exact details of what God wanted. So he started with the clear will of God: *Go, preach the gospel in all the world.* He took this general command and chose a way he could practically implement it. Yes, I'm sure he prayed first, but we know from the record that Paul's prayers didn't exempt him from having to forge ahead without customized directions.

He spent time, money, emotions, and work doing by principle what had not yet been revealed to him by revelation. Or in other words, sometimes you don't get the big unmistakable, "Whoa, that was awesome!" confirmation that you are in God's will until after you have tried to go into Asia and Bithynia, so to speak.

Your Asia and Bithynia may be taking a timid step toward what you think may be God's will. What if you're wrong? So what if you are wrong? Was Paul *wrong* for taking a step toward Bithynia and later Asia?

Did God reprimand him for using his initiative in the absence of customized instructions? No. He blessed him as long as he followed His general will. And when Paul's initiative, which was in submission to God, brought him to a place God didn't want him, God spoke clearly.

God is a fantastic communicator. If you get to a place where you are about to make a so-called *wrong* decision, whether it stems from your humanity or sinfulness, He'll talk to you, too.

God Doesn't Expect You to Know Everything When You Pray

Here is something that has helped me and others hugely in our prayers. Paul was wrong only in the sense that he was human, and humans don't know everything. Please hear and never forget this: God doesn't expect you to know everything—even as you pray.

I like to tell people that failure is built into the system, and it doesn't bother God one bit. I get this concept from the entire Bible, but specifically from 1 Corinthians 13:9, 12. Here it says we see through a glass, darkly, and we have only partial knowledge and partial effectiveness in spiritual gifts. Call it what you will, but this sounds like the perfect recipe for a bunch of mistakes and a bunch of unanswered questions.

Don't worry about this context of imperfection we're in. It's just the way it is. It'll be this way until the Lord returns. Drop to your knees. Submit yourself to God in humility. Tell Him you don't have all the facts you'd like to have, but you're going to use what you do have to make your petition.

You know that God is holy, righteous, just, loving, kind, and forgiving. You know that for some reason He has this crazy, irrational love for you. You know that the Scripture says, "The eyes of the Lord are upon the righteous, and His ears are open to their cry," (Psalm 34:15). You know that He has told you to "come boldly to the throne of grace, that we may obtain mercy and find grace to help in time of need" (Hebrews 4:16).

God has set this thing up so that His glory and power is manifested through imperfect and often bumbling misfits who dare to trust Him to do the impossible. Soon you'll be able to say with the psalmist, "I sought the Lord, and He heard me, and delivered me from all my fears" (Psalm 34:4).

Come on, son or daughter of God. You can do it!

Lessons Learned

Lesson One. The answer to my prayer may already be revealed in the Bible.

Lesson Two. Prayer paralysis is often caused by forgetting to use some of the principles we successfully use every day as we make decisions.

Lesson Three. If I don't know the *exact* will of God, I ca confidently follow the general will of God and what I know about Him until He chooses to reveal more details. M confidence in prayer is not in knowing exact details, but i knowing God.

Lesson Four. God doesn't hold my humanity against me a I pray. I can boldly go to the throne of grace to get help eve when I don't know as much as I'd like to know about th situation or exact details in God's heart.

Practical Exercise

Pray out loud: "Lord, I don't know as much as I'd like t know about this situation, but I now know You don't expec me to know everything. Though I offer You my prayers wit imperfect knowledge, I have faith that You hear me. As I pray I'm watching and listening for any further light from You. Unt I receive more, I will pray in faith with what I have."

Chapter Five
Commit to Change the Situation through Prayer

"Now about that time Herod the king stretched out his hand to harass some from the church. Then he killed James the brother of John with the sword. And because he saw that it pleased the Jews, he proceeded further to seize Peter also...Peter was therefore kept in prison, but constant prayer was offered to God for him by the church."

Acts 12:1-3, 5

We know that prayer is our most powerful weapon. We preach it. We teach it. We speak it. We sing it. We write it. Nonetheless, often it's either the last thing done, the thing done with little duration, or the thing done not at all. What's going on? Are we lazy? Negligent? Unbelieving?

Certainly, I know there are moments like these and people like this. This book's intent, however, isn't to beat up on people; so, I'll let God handle any reprimands. Rather, I want to help those who know, or possibly only have an inkling, that prayer can help their situation, yet find themselves not praying. These people aren't lazy, negligent, or unbelieving. There's something else going on here.

Busyness, Tiredness, and Past Prayer Failures
Can Steal Prayer Time

There have been times when I planned to pray and later got so busy doing stuff that by the time I finished, I was exhausted. I'd either press through and get on my knees and promptly fall asleep, or I'd try to outsmart my tiredness by prayer walking in my room. Often that only transformed me from a lying mummy to a walking zombie! Not a lot accomplished.

I haven't yet figured out how to be absolutely dead tired and pray with any real energy or duration. *B...u...u...t* I have discovered something useful. If I really want to pray, I have to deliberately take steps now to either not be dead tired later, or change my prayer time from later to now.

What Can You Stop, Start, or Modify to Save Time?

Write or type a list of your daily activities. Which are fixed and which are not? For instance, are you married? Do you have children? What about other obligations that aren't going anywhere? Now do the same with activities where you have more discretion. How often do you do these things? For how long? Is there anything you can stop, start, or modify that will give you more time to pray? Can you cut sixty minutes a day? Thirty? Ten?

Do you know how much more powerful you would be in prayer if you offered ten more minutes a day of intelligent prayer to your heavenly Father who is just itching to show you His mighty power? Did you know that ten minutes a day comes out to sixty hours a year? The last thing Satan wants is for you to spend sixty hours in the presence of God your Father!

Maybe this short list will give you some practical ideas of how to find time to pray. Ask yourself can you stop, start, or modify any of these activities: cooking, cleaning, talking on the phone, surfing the web, reading, watching television, shopping, eating, sleeping, visiting, working, vacationing, lawn work, hobbies, etc. Believe God for ideas. If you want to pray, He'll help you find time.

Or perhaps your best course of action is to simply pray now rather than later. Can you pray as you drive to and from work? Driving to work is better than driving from work because now is always better than later. Can you go to the restroom and pray? I've had many, many, *many* awesome prayer sessions in the restroom. If you did this two or three times a day, you'd have significant breakthroughs in prayer. Can you get up earlier so you can pray? Next time you're running an errand, can you pull over somewhere safe and cry out to God in prayer? You get the picture. Be aggressive and use your imagination. You won't regret it!

Don't Let Yesterday's Prayer Failure Stop You From Today's Prayer Answer

If we define prayer failure as praying for something specific and spectacularly *not* getting it, then there's nothing like a prayer failure to discourage you from praying like that again. It's at this point that we cut back on praying. Or we may do the downward adjustment thing and only pray in safe, general terms. Nothing too specific. Nothing that will by its failure to come or refusal to go can embarrass us or damage our faith any more than it's already damaged.

But in what field or industry do we find successful people who haven't had to deal with setbacks, disappointments, and failures? As part of your quest toward regular answered prayers, and even spectacular prayer answers, you must learn to get off the mat and stand on your feet again. Okay, so you prayed for something and things didn't turn out the way you hoped they would. Join the club. We've all been there. This changes nothing about the power, influence, and creativity of God to answer your next prayer.

The story in our opening Scriptures tell of a church crisis that was conquered through prayer. The apostle James was unjustly put in prison for his faith in Christ. I have to believe the church prayed for him. We're talking eleven other apostles and thousands of converts in an on fire church. It would be a real stretch to assume they didn't pray. And if they didn't, James probably did. Wouldn't you? Nonetheless, James was executed! This is big time prayer failure.

Next, King Herod put Peter in prison for the same purpose. "But constant prayer was offered to God for him by the church." God sent His angel and delivered Peter. That's way beyond awesome. But here's what's also awesome. The church had just experienced a spectacular prayer failure. They had every reason in the world to throw in the prayer towel and say, "We prayed for James and his head is rolling down the street like a bowling ball. This stuff doesn't work. I'm going back to praying for empty parking spaces at the mall."

Instead, they refused to focus on their shock, grief, and unanswered questions. They focused instead on the unchanging character of God, and on His power, influence, and creativity to answer prayers. Son or daughter of God, you may have suffered devastating prayer failures, but God is still on the throne and Satan is still defeated. You don't need to have every question answered before you get back in the win column.

What you do need is what the early church had. They trusted in God's faithfulness and radically rearranged their schedules to offer prayer sufficient to meet the newest crisis. Let yesterday's failure drive you to even greater levels of prayer!

Lessons Learned

Lesson One. I can ask God to help me examine my daily activities for areas I can start, stop, or modify things that will give me more time to pray. Even ten more minutes a day is sixty hours a year in the presence of God!

Lesson Two. Yesterday's spectacular prayer failure doesn't mean there aren't many spectacular prayer answers in my future!

Practical Exercise

Pray, "Lord, what can I start, stop, or modify that will give me more time to pray." Now with your eyes closed, wait before the Lord for a little while. Write down the thoughts that come.

Chapter Six

Sometimes a Sense of Urgency Is Needed to Change the Situation

*"Therefore I say to you, whatever
things you ask when you pray,
believe that you receive them, and
you shall have them."*

Mark 11:24

This promise is a continuation of Jesus telling us to speak to our mountains in faith and they will move. There is something both fascinating and critical I want you to understand about this promise. The word "ask," or "desire" as some versions use, is different from what we might suppose. The word Jesus used, *aiteo*, includes the idea of a craving that might cause one to beg.

The point is not that we must beg God in the sense that we're trying to get Him to do something He doesn't want to do. It is that when we pray, we need to understand that what He considers asking may be quite different than our definition.

Window Shopping Is Not Praying

For instance, a young child may walk down the aisle of a store and see the bright colors and point to item after item saying, "I want that!" The smart parent keeps walking until the interest dies down. Adults have fleeting interests, too.

Have you ever gone window shopping? "Oh, that's beautiful. I'd love to have that," you say, but you keep walking.

When God says we can get what we desire through prayer, He specifically excluded window shopping type prayers. This doesn't mean He won't often lavish you with a love gift that's way out of proportion to your obedience, faith, or prayer. (I mean, my goodness, what is salvation?) But as a general rule, He doesn't answer prayers that don't originate from a strong desire. There are a few reasons for this.

First, mountains or strongholds by definition are too stubborn to yield to prayers that lack a desire strong enough to keep the praying person praying. Think of Daniel needing to hold on in intense prayer for twenty-one days before the answer came (Daniel 10:1-14).

Second, this brief life is our training ground for eternity, and He uses our prayers as part of the training. We may not think of it often or seriously contemplate ruling and reigning with Christ throughout eternity on the new Earth, but He is dead serious about this. Everything He does in regard to our prayers is within the context of Him conforming us to the image of His dear Son, Jesus Christ, and of us ruling with Him.

The significance of this is He never passes up an opportunity to further us along in our spiritual growth. Every prayer is answered, delayed, or denied within the context of growing us up and getting us ready for eternity.

We see through a glass, darkly, and we have partial knowledge. So, no matter how wonderful our motives or dire our situation, we nearly always pray from a position of deficiency. So how is this deficiency overcome? How can God grant mountain moving, world changing power to people in this compromised, often sinful, condition?

My understanding is that since we often operate at such an acute deficit of knowledge (or character or faith or love or a hundred other things!) when we pray, we come before Him boldly as sons and daughters, but are nonetheless in utter dependence upon His goodness and wisdom to bring whatever we pray for to pass. And a tool He uses to overcome our deficit is the time interval between the prayer request and its answer. *Time is a tool in the hands of God when we are praying.*

How God Uses Urgency and Time
to Answer Our Prayers

No matter how dire the situation or noble our interest, when we pray God's primary concern is answering the prayer in such a way that you are transformed. This normally takes time. However, if there's not enough desire, or urgency, in your heart for the object you're praying for, chances are you won't hang around long enough for God's work to be done in your heart.

Unless God decides otherwise, this often results in what appears as God saying no to your request. Actually, He's not saying, "No." He's saying, "Get yourself back in here so we can finish the transformation process in your heart. You need to be changed so I can answer the prayer."

If you stay in prayer long enough, the Holy Spirit will search your heart and bring thoughts to your mind. These thoughts will give you a portion of God's perspective on whatever you're praying for. They'll also reveal to you things about yourself. This is a coveted place to be! It's the transformation process. If you respond honestly and patiently to these thoughts, you will be changed and barriers to your prayers will disappear.

And as I said when I opened this chapter, some situations are so complicated or so reinforced with demonic power that only sustained prayer power will secure the victory. *Sustained prayer.* Just another way of saying desire or urgency.

How to Get More Urgency

Since urgency is often needed for our prayer to qualify as true prayer from God's perspective, how do we get more urgency? Good news, it's not a matter of will power. If it were, most of us would be in permanent trouble because creating willpower is like grasping fog in your hand.

Time to smile. There is a backdoor way to get urgency without short-lived, exhausting efforts of trying to will yourself into it. The secret is to use the right tool. Who changes a tire by using brute force to lift the car off the ground? We use a car jack that allows us to lift thousands of pounds with relatively little effort. Similarly, there is a prayer tool that lifts our urgency level higher than we ever could by will power alone. That tool is exposure to something that *automatically* produces urgency.

The Bible is filled with examples of people getting spectacular answers to prayers that required great intensity, focus...*urgency*. None of these people tried to manufacture urgency. Let's look at one of them to get an idea of what I'm talking about.

Hannah (1 Samuel 1:1-20). Hannah's prayers overcame her infertility. Hannah didn't try to have urgency. Nor did she try to pray longer or more regularly. Her urgency, length, and regularity in prayer came automatically by what she was exposed to. *She was constantly exposed to the daily taunting of a human tormentor, which aggravated her sense of loss and drove her to her knees.*

Do you really want more urgency in prayer? You want to pray longer and with more focus. Be like Hannah. Allow your circumstance to drive you to your knees. But what if you don't have a daily tormentor like Hannah, so to speak? Something like pain or immediate danger to make you get off the internet or turn off the TV? What if you just want more urgency, duration, and focus when you pray about regular stuff?

Is the regular stuff important? How important? What happens to the object of your prayer if you don't pray? If the perceived repercussions of not praying aren't serious to you, you're not going to have a sense of urgency. Conversely, if you feel there's a chance of something bad happening by you not praying, you will find a sense of uneasiness inside of you. What you want is to inflame that sense of unease to a strength level that displaces your other time-eating priorities—at least for a while.

You can increase the sense of unease by deliberately putting before your face things that make you think about the object you desire to pray about. You want to pray about someone more regularly? Put their name on your prayer list. Look at their name as you pray. Better yet, use a picture of them if you can. You want to pray for them more urgently? As positive as you might be, make yourself think of worse case scenarios concerning them. Now pray.

I know how that last statement sounds. So let me give you an example that hopefully will put my statement in context. You're praying for someone's salvation, but not with any real sense of regularity, duration, or urgency. *Make yourself think of what happens if this person isn't saved.* There's only heaven or hell. The prospect of someone spending eternity in that horrible place will automatically help you pray for them—if you think on it honestly. You can do this for anything you're praying about.

Finally, perhaps Jesus's own words will help clarify. Jesus said, "Blessed are the poor in spirit...blessed are those who mourn..." (Matthew 5:3, 4). The blessing is not in simply being poor in spirit or of mourning. The blessing is that the person knows he's poor in spirit. When you know you're poor in spirit, it produces a spiritual mourning. The end result is you're driven to Jesus by a revelation of your need.

Now apply the concept of what Jesus said to whatever it is you're praying about. Just as a sinner is driven to Jesus by an awareness of his spiritual poverty, you can be driven to Jesus by an awareness of spiritual poverty. The poverty is, *What is the present condition of my prayer object? What is the worst case scenario of my prayer object if the situation doesn't change?*

Now just as the sinner must think on his condition honestly enough and long enough for the Holy Spirit to change his heart, you, too, must do the same. You will find your heart getting softer and your emotions getting stirred.

If this still seems a little on the negative side for you, do the exact opposite (whatever works!). Think on the good that can happen if you keep praying. Either way...

Here comes urgency!

Lessons Learned

Lesson One. God wants to see real desire in my prayers. If I am only window shopping, I will modify and intelligently increase my desire.

Lesson Two. I will remember that God uses the time interval between the prayer and the answer to grow me up into the image of Christ and to prepare me to rule and reign with Him on the new Earth throughout eternity.

Lesson Three. I will stop wearing myself out in the flesh trying to be a better prayer warrior, and will instead increase my sense of urgency in prayer by using the tool of honest exposure to the need. I will remember how it worked for Hannah in 1 Samuel 1:1-20).

Practical Exercise

Pray, *Lord, I know that every prayer doesn't require me to pour out my soul. And I know that You love me, and that You're*

so kind and longsuffering that You often answer prayers eve
when we should pray better. But I know that some thing
require more fervency and urgency in prayer.

I'm going to do my best to expose myself to things tha
remind me of the importance of this prayer being answered
Will You please help me in this? I know You will; so I thank Yo
now that my sense of urgency in prayer is growing.

Chapter Seven
Quote the Word of God Out Loud to Yourself, to Satan, and to God

"For the word of God is alive and powerful, sharper than any two-edged sword, piercing even to the division of soul and spirit, and of joints and marrow, and is a discerner of the thoughts and intents of the heart."

Hebrews 4:12

One of the most powerful things you can do as you pray is to quote the word of God to yourself, to Satan, and to God. I did it when I defied the housing market and sold my home quickly for full price. I've done it for other crises, and I do it for regular prayers. My friends who get their prayers answered, do it too. The Bible is filled with examples of people successfully using the spoken Word as a powerful prayer tool.

Quote the Word to Yourself

Here are some reasons you should quote the word of God to yourself out loud as you pray:

1. It reminds you of God's faithfulness.
2. It honors God in the presence of the holy angels and of the demonic forces just as Job honored God.
3. It can help keep your mind focused.

4. It helps to fill up dead air when you want to say more in prayer, but don't know what to say.

Quote the Word to Satan

Here are some reasons you should quote the word of God to Satan out loud as you pray:

1. It is literally alive with God's power when it is released from the mouth of a son or daughter of God.
2. It is called by the Holy Spirit "the sword of the Spirit" (Ephesians 6:17).
3. It was used by Jesus in the wilderness to defeat the devil.

Quote the Word to God

Here are some reasons you should quote the word of God to Him out loud as you pray:

1. It puts you on extremely safe ground as you explain your case and press for an answer (more about this later).
2. It is the foundation of His kingdom and the spiritual force that holds all things together (Hebrews 1:3).
3. It pleases God when you use His Word in your prayers (Isaiah 43:26; John 15:7).

A Clarification About Quoting God's Word to Him

Depending upon what Christian circles in which you travel, you may hear that you can use the Word of God to "command" God or to obligate Him to give you what you pray for, especially if you have enough faith. For instance, Isaiah 45:11 has the phrase, "concerning the work of My hands, you command Me."

Ordinarily, the silliness of a created, finite being, who only partially sees and knows, and who is totally dependent upon his Creator for his breath, heartbeat, and brainwave, using this or any Scripture to support the belief that he can obligate God to do anything should be comically obvious as foolish. So, I won't waste space explaining why the ice cube doesn't control the sun.

But this errant word of faith heresy originated with a seed of truth. So we must be careful not to discard the truth with the error. The truth is that God voluntarily shares His authority and power with us. This isn't a charismatic or word of faith doctrine. This is a Bible truth that transcends denominations and Christian doctrine fads.

It started in Genesis with Adam and Eve. We see it clearly in the Old Testament with God delegating authority and power to kings, priests, and prophets. We see it clearly in the New Testament with God delegating authority and power first to Jesus (the eternal Word made flesh), then with Christ delegating authority and power to the twelve disciples, then with Christ delegating His authority and power to every single son and daughter of God.

No amount of silliness or presumption or abuse can or ever will reverse God's decision to share His authority and power with His people. He "has made us kings and priests to His God and Father..." (Revelation 1:6).

Our Success in Prayer Depends Totally On His Sovereignty

Nonetheless, we are kings and priests on a leash. The leash is God's sovereignty. No amount of quoting God's word to Him circumvents His discretion as God. When we quote God's word to Him, it is not to control Him the way someone may control a genie after rubbing the bottle.

If we are to successfully speak God's own promises to Him during prayer, we must understand that this whole process is one of grace on His part and not leverage on our part. He invites us in our knowledge and understanding deficit to participate in His rule of the world through prayer. He encourages and honors initiative and boldness in prayer that is only accurately conceivable within the context of His immeasurable and unfathomable mercy, patience, and love.

Yet there is nothing about His invitation for us to pray that compromises His position as God. He has final approval and veto authority over every prayer—irrespective of any spiritual effort on our part. Therefore, our boldness in prayer as sons and daughters is tempered with deep humility, knowing that our loving Father is also our Creator, Sustainer, Savior, and God.

Lessons Learned

Lesson One. It is beneficial to quote the word of God to myself, to Satan, and to the Lord as I pray.

Lesson Two. God gives us incredible discretion in our prayer requests, but He maintains His right as the perfect Almighty God to delay, deny, or grant any of our requests.

Practical Exercise

1. Look on your list and find two or three Scriptures that cover those prayer requests.

2. Lift one hand above your head to God as you quote the Word to Him.

3. Place a hand over your heart as you quote the Word to yourself.

4. Point your finger defiantly toward the floor as you quote the Word to the devil.

Chapter Eight
Speak to the Mountain in Faith

*"Assuredly, I say to you, if you have
faith and do not doubt, you will not
only do what was done to the fig
tree, but also if you say to this
mountain, 'Be removed and be cast
into the sea,' it will be done. And
whatever things you ask in prayer,
believing, you will receive."*

Matthew 21:21, 22

Often adding or omitting a simple ingredient causes something remarkable to happen that is disproportionate to the relative size of the ingredient. Often that ingredient is so simple that prior to its addition, it's overlooked for its simplicity, or it's scorned for its ridiculousness. *Speaking directly to your mountain is one such ingredient.*

Could it be that the mountain that has been resisting your prayer efforts is waiting for you to add the simple ingredient of talking to it in Jesus's name? Could it be that God's answer to your prayer is not, "No," but, "Obey Matthew 21:21"? Too simple? Too ridiculous? If you think so, consider that the entirety of Christian faith is based upon eternal truths that are simple and ridiculous.

Sinners stumble over the gospel because of its simplicity. "That if you confess with your mouth the Lord Jesus and believe in your heart that God has raised Him from the dead, you will be saved" (Romans 10:9). *Believe in your hear* *confess with your mouth.* Extraordinarily simple an extraordinarily ridiculous. Paul said the Jews couldn't accep it because it was too pragmatically simple—they wante something hard to work for. The Greeks couldn't accept because it was too philosophically simple—they wante something complicated they'd have to figure out.

What about you? Does Matthew 21:21 offend you? Is too simple and ridiculous? You've prayed, cried, moanee screamed, fasted, and quoted the Word. And now here some guy telling you it's possible that the mountain will finall obey once you start orally commanding it to obey you? Ye the Bible is full of examples of people moving mountains b speaking to them.

Let's Face It, Speaking to Mountains Is Foolish ...Yet It Works!

I regularly use this spiritual tool in my healing ministr Most of the healings I've seen have come about as I spok directly to the condition. Yet I have a confession to make Even after many years of seeing people healed this way, I st often *feel* foolish when I speak to mountains, especially others are present watching me. How can I not feel foolis speaking to someone's limb or spine? So what do I do? I obe Matthew 21:21 irrespective of how foolish it seems. Isn't th what we do with all the other so-called "foolish" parts of th Bible?

Briefly, here's a list of Bible examples of peopl successfully conquering mountains by speaking to them. I omit Jesus because we already know He can do this. We nee to see that His followers can do it, too.

Joshua needed sunlight to fight against the enemies Israel. He commanded the sun not to go down and it obeye (Joshua 10:7-14). Ezekiel made the valley of dry bones live b speaking to them (Ezekiel 37:1-14). The Twelve disciples made demons leave people (and thus affecting healing in their minds and bodies) by commanding them to leave (Mark 6:7-13). Seventy disciples other than the Twelve spoke to demons and made them leave people (Luke 10:1-17). An unnamed disciple other than one of the Twelve spoke to demons and healed people in this way (Mark 9:38-40). Peter raised a dead woman to life by praying first and then speaking to her dead body (Acts 9:36-42).

Perhaps you're not dealing with a demon, a dead body, or a valley filled with dry bones. That's okay. We all have our own situations. Whatever yours is, add Matthew 21:21 to your prayer tool box and see what happens. You may be in for a spectacular surprise!

Lessons Learned

Lesson. My mountain may be waiting for me to speak to it before it will leave!

Practical Exercise

1. Pick something on your prayer list.

2. Speak Matthew 21:21, 22 to it. Tell it that it's nothing but a mountain and that Jesus said you could move mountains.

3. Use your own words to speak to the mountain. Authoritatively tell it to leave or change or whatever you need it to do. Remember: You don't need to know how this will happen. In fact, if you can figure it out, it's probably not a mountain.

4. According to Matthew 21: 22, pray, "Lord, I have spoken to the mountain and I know that You are

releasing Your power in my behalf as I stand in faith.
But I know the mountain is still literally there and I
must practically deal with its natural reality until it
obeys.

Chapter Nine
Pray With Fervency and Tears

*"The earnest (heartfelt, continued)
prayer of a righteous man makes
tremendous power available
[dynamic in its working]."*

James 5:16 (Amplified Bible)

Successful prayer comes in all forms. Short. Long. Silent. Loud. Calm. Passionate. Private. Public. And none of their presentations is what alone makes them successful. It isn't its length or loudness alone that causes a prayer to be granted. As this little book posits, it's the combination of several things. Fervency and tears are two of those ingredients.

We've spoken in another place of fervency under the name *urgency*. They're one and the same. Here we'll look at one of the natural fruits of fervency—tears. Tears come from emotion. God created emotion and emotion is good. Of course, it can also be bad in an undisciplined or perverted state. But we're talking about good emotions helping us to pray more effectively.

Emotion Adds Power to Our Prayers
Because God is Emotional

Some prayers require tears. Hot bitter tears accompanied with awkward gushings of pain that escape from your mouth as groans. I do not speak of emotionalism; you doing something to whip yourself up into a frenzy. What I'm speaking of is natural, automatic. It's what comes out of your heart because there is no way to keep it in. *Emotion that demands an outlet.*

The Scripture used above speaks of tremendous power made available through the saint's fervent, or *heartfelt and continued*, prayers. How do we know they're fervent? Because they're continued. Why do they continue? Because the heart has been gripped. By what? Emotion. And why is emotion so important to successful prayer? Because God is emotional, and he expects emotion from you. Again, not emotionalism, emotion. *The outward expression of what is in your heart.*

God Desires You to Be Emotional With Him When You Pray

Read the Bible with the intent of observing God's emotions and you'll soon discover He's exceedingly emotional. Not exceedingly unstable, imbalanced, or unpredictable—emotional...*feeling.* God speaks descriptively of His anger, hatred, joy, and love from Genesis to Revelation.

Often, we fall prey to our sophisticated western culture or unemotional church tradition and reserve strong outward displays of emotions to sporting events and funerals. Despite being loved of God, forgiven of our sins, delivered from eternal damnation, adopted into God's family, given eternal life, and awaiting the promise of the glorious kingdom of God, we are careful not to allow these wonderful things to cause us to show too much emotion in a church setting. If we do, we are promptly classified as Pentecostal or said to be given to emotionalism, which, *of course*, is bad.

That's tragic enough, but we carry the tragedy to a new level when we get before God in prayer with this subdued behavior. He desires a passionate relationship with His family, not a series of dry, formal transactions of supplicant unemotionally begging a cold, far off deity. Indeed, He commands us to "love the Lord thy God with all of your heart, with all of your soul, with all of your mind, and with all of your strength" (Mark 12:30). Heart, mind, soul, strength. Emotions are covered in there somewhere. *So He actually commands us to be emotional with Him!*

Emotions Helped the Prophet Elijah Get His Prayers Answered

The Scriptures at the top of the page (James 5:13-18) encourage sick Christians to call for the elders of the church. The elders are told that if they pray like Elijah, spectacular answers can happen. They're also told that "Elijah was a man with a nature like ours, and he prayed earnestly that it would not rain, and it did not rain...and he prayed again, and the heaven gave rain..." Or in other words, don't look at Elijah like he's a one of a kind prayer warrior. Instead, copy him and get similar results! (Read 1 Kings 17:1-7; 18:41-45 for the full story).

When you consider what the Scriptures say about Elijah in 1 Kings and James, you find that the back story of his requests reveals a mountain. He was the only prophet in the nation publicly challenging the apostate king and his murderous wife. There was a death warrant out for him. He simply couldn't afford not to get his prayers answered! So he prayed earnestly, fervently. When his first six prayer sessions failed to produce rain, his emotion drove him to pray again. Prayer seven brought the rain.

Read the story again. Elijah's life was literally at stake. We know he prayed emotionally because emotion is part of fervency. God instructed us to pray like Elijah for spectacular results, didn't He? This means we may have to adjust how we view emotion in prayer. Now let's see some examples where tears are clearly a part of emotion.

Jesus Offered His Prayers with Strong Cries and Many Tears

On the night He was betrayed, Jesus prayed in th wilderness with great emotion, great earnestness. "And bein in agony, He prayed more earnestly. Then His sweat becam like great drops of blood falling down to the ground" (Luk 22:44). Surprisingly, this was *after* an angel had strengthene Him. So what must He have been going through prior to bein strengthened by the angel? Talk about intensity!

Did the Lord's emotional prayer include tears? Glad yo asked. "...Who in the days of His flesh, when He had offere up prayers and supplications, *with vehement cries and tear* to Him who was able to save Him from death..." (Hebrew 5:7). Not only did He cry, He cried vehemently with tears. Th means His cries were loud and filled with the energy c desperation and agony. His face was filled with tears!

A Dying Man Who Offered Prayers with Fervency and Tears

King Hezekiah was given a death sentence by God Himse Case closed, right? Hezekiah didn't think so. "Then he turne his face toward the wall, and prayed to the Lord...and [durin prayer] Hezekiah wept bitterly" (2 Kings 20:2, 3). How did th affect God? "I have heard your prayer, I have seen your tear surely I will heal you" (2 Kings 20:5).

Did you see it? The dying king was able to change God mind through fervent prayers offered with tears. Were th tears important? Could the prayer have been answere without them? No need to guess. The Scriptures say, "I hav heard your prayers. I have seen your tears." Evidently, th king's tears made as much an impression on God as h prayers. Never underestimate the power of tears offered un

God. He is an emotional God, and He wants you to share your emotions with Him.

God Calls Us to Offer Sincere Tears with Our Prayers

God commanded His people through the prophet Joel to "Turn to Me with all your heart, with fasting, with weeping, and with mourning...rend your heart...weep between the porch and the altar...Then the Lord will be zealous for His land, and pity His people" (Joel 2:12, 13, 17-19).

Fervency and sincere tears mean much to the Lord, first, because He is emotional (He created emotion), and second, because He knows that prayers not offered with emotion have not yet gripped our heart. Remember, "What things so ever you desire [crave to the point of begging], when you pray, believe that you receive them, and you shall have them" (Mark 11:24).

Let's add fervency and sincere tears to our prayers so we may have this testimony: "This poor man cried out, and the Lord heard him, and saved him out of all his troubles" (Psalm 34:6). Don't try to manufacture emotion or tears. Just let the mountain do its work. If there's no mountain, just get before your Father and think on Him and ask Him to unlock your emotions so you can pour out your heart to Him. Give the Holy Spirit enough time to do this and He will. And when He comes, don't be shy!

Lessons Learned

Lesson One. Emotion adds power to my prayers because God is emotional.

Lesson Two. God commands me to have an emotional relationship with Him (Mark 12:30).

Lesson Three. Sincere tears mean a lot to God.

Practical Exercise

1. Pick something on the list that is worthy of emotion.

2. Ask God to convert your desire for this thing into emotion that can be used in prayer.

3. Wait before God for a while and give Him time to touch your heart.

4. If you go a good while and feel nothing, don't be condemned! This is part of the process. Instead turn your lack of emotion into a good prayer. Pray something like this: "Lord, this thing I'm praying for is really serious. I can't afford for this prayer to go unanswered. Yet I know that you said, 'The effective fervent prayer of a righteous man makes great power available.' I feel I don't have the fervency I need. Why, Lord? Why don't I have it? Why doesn't this thing grip my heart? Help me, Lord." And just continue in this way until something happens. Celebrate the slightest increase of emotion you discern!

5. Thank God for your increased emotions—even if you haven't yet discerned an increase. It's coming. People of faith thank God before they see the answer to their prayers. And whether you feel like it or not, you're a person of faith!

Chapter Ten

Talk to God in Great Detail About the Mountain...Again and Again

"Trust in Him at all times, you people; pour out your heart before Him; God is a refuge for us."

Psalm 62:8

Successful prayer often requires that we pour out our heart before God. Some people are reluctant to do this because they feel God already knows their needs. Why tell Him something He already knows? Others will do it once, but not more than once. Wouldn't it be unbelief to bring up the same issue again? That's what some faith teachers tell us.

Obviously, the Lord knows our situation better than we do. We can't tell Him anything He doesn't already know. But we miss the point. Prayer is never to enlighten God. It is to enlighten us, and to involve us in the influencing and changing of affairs of this life. That's part of our growth as future co-rulers of God's creation. It is also to worship the Lord and to build an intimate relationship with Him.

And what about talking to Him about the same issue over and over? We do so for the same reasons I just listed. Additionally, we do it because the mountain we talked to Him about yesterday is still staring us in the face today.

Jesus Repeatedly Poured Out His Heart to God About the Same Issue

Jesus often spent whole nights in prayer. Or He'd get up hours before daylight and pray until one of his late sleeping disciples interrupted Him. I don't know how you'd pray that long, repeatedly, and not cover the same ground. But we don't have to guess whether or not He repeated Himself. We have the biblical record of His prayers the night he was betrayed.

> "Then He said to them [His disciples], 'My soul is exceedingly sorrowful, even to death. Stay here and watch [pray] with Me.' He went a little farther and fell on His face, and prayed, saying, 'O My Father, if it is possible, let this cup pass from Me; nevertheless, not as I will, but as You will.' Then He came to the disciples and found them sleeping, and said to Peter, 'What? Could you not watch with Me one hour? Watch and pray, lest you enter into temptation...

> Again, *a second time*, He went away and prayed, saying, 'O My Father, if this cup cannot pass away from Me unless I drink it, Your will be done.' And He came and found them asleep again, for their eyes were heavy.

So He left them, went away again,
*and prayed the third time, saying
the same words."*

Matthew 26:40-44

You see? Jesus prayed for the same thing three times, even saying the same words. What drove Him to pray with such persistence? He said it was because "My soul is exceedingly sorrowful, even to death." Spiritual and mental anguish drove Him to pour out His heart. But didn't He pour out His heart to the all-knowing God the first time?

Yes, but the mountain and the emotional pain were still there after the first prayer. So He prayed again. It was there after the second prayer, so He prayed again. After the third prayer, He was ready to face the mountain. In His case, the mountain was to be turned over to His enemies and to endure the cross and temporary separation from the Father.

This is where some people miss the mark in prayer. They don't honestly pour out their heart to God as Jesus did. They opt instead to let their religious tradition or quiet disposition shut them down prematurely. So they're never able to "Cast your burden on the Lord, and He shall sustain you" (Psalm 55:22). They're left spiritually and emotionally constipated.

Or they pour out their heart once and are convinced that's all it takes. Hey, sometimes that is all it takes. But more often than not, the mountain requires more prayer. The sad thing is many people feel in their gut that the job's not done. Their instincts tell them to do like Jesus and to go back to the Father and pour out the burden until it's no longer on them. Nonetheless, they've been taught that it's a bad thing to talk to God more than once about the same problem.

These people often try to *faith* it. That is, they try to have faith that the mountain is taken care of. They try to ignore the

nagging, often tormenting feeling that the mountain hasn'
been adequately dealt with. They try to cover these doubt
(spiritual realities, really) with positive words. But faithing
when the mountain hasn't been adequately dealt with
actually *faking* it. And at the base of the mountain is
graveyard full of fakes.

Jesus had an overwhelming problem the evening of Hi
betrayal. He didn't say, "Well, My Father knows what I'r
going through. I'm going to sleep." Nor did He say, "I'v
prayed once about this situation. I'm not praying about
again. I'll ignore my gut feeling and just speak positive." Ha
He done either of these...well, I don't even want to go there

When You Pray, Do Not Use Vain Repetitions
As the Heathen Do

Some people don't pour out their hearts to God becaus
they misunderstand Matthew 6:7, 8: "And when you pray, d
not use vain repetitions as the heathen do. For they think tha
they will be heard for their many words. Therefore do not b
like them. For your Father knows the things you have need o
before you ask Him."

Somehow they equate "Do not use vain repetitions" as *D
not pray for the same thing more than once.* And othe
equate "For your Father knows the things you have need o
before you ask Him" as *Don't ask Him for anything, since H
already knows what you need.* But Jesus wasn't telling the
to pray once and quit praying. And He certainly wasn't tellin
them not to pray at all! Jesus was simply telling them how t
pray more effectively.

The heathen do not know God. They try to make up wit
words what they lack in relationship. So they offer a bunch o
words. Perhaps *special* words. Their hope is in their word
not in the god to whom the words are addressed.

This error is also committed by well-meaning Christians who trust more in the power of their words than the intelligence of God. They are so afraid of unleashing negative forces by speaking what they feel are negative words that they can't be honest with God. When they do talk to God, it's in the code language of a positive confession. Yes, the positive confession should become part of your prayers. But not before you speak to God with brutal honesty about the problem (Isn't that how Jesus prayed?). Only in this way will the doubts of your heart be uprooted and your confession of faith be anchored in spiritual reality rather than wishful or delusional thinking.

God is intelligent beyond your wildest imagination. He knows the difference between someone choosing to stay in unbelief and someone praying themselves out of unbelief. Never fear talking to Him about the mountain in great detail, even if you have to do it more than once, and even if it sounds like unbelief. At this point in the prayer, it may be, and that's okay! This is how you get rid of unbelief.

Bottom line. Never, never, never have more faith in your words than in your God. You are not dealing with a divine formula or system to be mastered or manipulated. You are dealing with the God who "has made the earth by His power, He has established the world by His wisdom, and stretched out the heavens with His understanding" (Jeremiah 10:12).

And what of the belief that we shouldn't ask God for anything because He already knows our need? The fallacy of this position is both obvious and indefensible. If we follow this reasoning to its logical conclusion, we shouldn't talk to God about anything! For He knows everything!

Come on. Let's put these bad doctrines behind us and pray before our Father with such liberty that we enter His courts with great burdens, fears, and unbelief and exit with great freedom, peace, and faith.

Lessons Learned

Lesson One. I will follow Jesus's example and pour out my heart and talk to God about the mountain until the burden rolls off of me and onto Him.

Lesson Two. Prayer is not to tell God something He doesn't already know. It's for me to share in the process of His solution, and to build a relationship with Him.

Practical Exercise

Pour out your heart to God about something on your prayer list. Talk to Him in great detail about it. Then talk to Him again and again about it. This isn't because He's hard of hearing. It's because He loves the time of fellowship with you. It's also because this is how you roll your cares over onto the Lord.

Chapter Eleven

Praise God During and After the Prayer

"Be anxious for nothing, but in everything by prayer and supplication, with thanksgiving, let your requests be made known to God; and the peace of God, which surpasses all understanding, will guard your hearts and minds through Christ Jesus."

Philippians 4:6, 7

Praise and worship of God in the face of a mountain is one of the most powerful spiritual weapons in your prayer arsenal. There is nothing that shows greater appreciation of God, greater growth in Christ, and greater contempt of the devil.

I have had many opportunities (though they rarely *feel* like opportunities during the trial!) to exalt God while a mountain towered over me. I recall one occasion when I was facing a bad situation, horrible actually. From a natural perspective, I was completely at the mercy of the mountain. If God didn't come through for me, I was going to be swallowed whole by a financial crisis.

I did everything in this book, *plus* I lifted my hands and worshipped my Father. I told God that I was trusting in His almighty power to overrule men and to reverse the situation. But I went a step farther. I looked at my ceiling with my hands uplifted and by faith looked into the heavens to the very throne room of God. I said, "Father, I don't care how this turns out, I will worship You. I will praise You because of what You've already done for me. I don't serve You just because of what You give me. I serve You because You're God and You're worthy to be praised!"

I then defiantly pointed to the floor and by faith looked into the face of Satan himself and said, "Listen to me, devil! will never bow my knees to you! I will never curse God! No matter what happens, I will praise Him!"

That fiery trial lasted about a month, but it felt like a thousand years. Some of you know what I'm talking about. Trials can be exceedingly tormenting. Nonetheless, continued to praise Him in the face of the mountain and the Lord prevailed, and rather than being diminished, I was exalted.

Faith That Worships God in the Midst of the Trial Honors God and Releases Mighty Power

The story of the trial of the three Hebrew teenagers in Daniel 3 perfectly demonstrates what I'm talking about. The king had made a golden image and commanded everyone to bow down and worship before it under the threat of death. The three godly teens refused. King Nebuchadnezzar confronted them and gave them one last chance to obey or be cast into a burning furnace. Their answer was classic *worship in the face of a mountain* honor unto God.

> "...But if you do not worship, you
> shall be cast immediately into the
> midst of a burning fiery furnace.
> And who is the god who will deliver
> you from my hands? Shadrach,
> Meshach, and Abed-Nego
> answered and said to the king, 'O

*Nebuchadnezzar, we have no need
to answer you in this matter. If that
is the case, our God whom we
serve is able to save us from the
burning fiery furnace, and He will
deliver us from your hand, O king.
But if not, let it be known to you, O
king, that we do not serve your
gods, nor will we worship the gold
image which you have set up."*

v. 15-18

The end of this story is spectacular. They were thrown into the fire and the Lord joined them in the furnace and kept them from being burned. The teens exited the furnace and were promptly promoted. Good move, king.

Here's what you need to see for your own prayers. The Hebrew teens showed us two kinds of worship. The first is when they said, "Our God...is able to save us...and He will deliver us from your hand." The second is when they said, "But if not...we do not serve your gods, nor will we worship the gold image which you set up." The first is the kind of worship that says to the mountain, I serve a God who is worthy of my trust. The second says, "I serve a God who is worthy of my life."

The Hebrew teens showed great faith when they said they believed their God would deliver them. *God had not explicitly told them He would deliver them, but they knew it was a real possibility.* Yet they showed greater faith when they said they were prepared to die should He choose not to deliver them. *For the brutal fact was the furnace was real and their God had not told them they would be delivered.* This is the kind of worship that excites God to no end. For it shows that you

value Him above all else—even deliverance from th
mountain.

My final comment on this point is I call this faith *worshi*
because when we acknowledge God as Lord and spea
positively of His attributes, the Holy Spirit calls it worship (se
Matthew 8:1, 2).

Honor God and Strengthen Yourself
by Worshipping the Lord

Yet there is a place for more recognizable, tradition
worship during and after prayer. Paul and Silas had bee
unjustly put in prison. "But at midnight Paul and Silas wer
praying and singing hymns to God, and the prisoners wer
listening to them. Suddenly there was a great earthquake, s
that the foundations of the prison were shaken; an
immediately all the doors were opened and everyone's chair
were loosed" (Acts 16:25, 26).

I'm sure the apostles weren't praying and singing psalm
to God in the hopes that an earthquake would miraculous
free them from prison. Paul spent a lot of time in variou
prisons, and this is the only record we have of him bein
miraculously freed from any of them. The apostle
worshipped in the face of the mountain because that's wh
lovers of Christ do. We worship God...*because He's worthy!*

Lessons Learned

Lesson One. Praise and worship of God in the face of
mountain is one of the most powerful spiritual weapons in m
prayer arsenal.

Lesson Two. Faith that worships God in the midst of th
trial honors God and releases mighty power.

Practical Exercise

Lift your hands before the Lord and worship Him. Tell Him that you believe He is able to answer your prayers, and that in your limited knowledge you believe He will answer. Then tell Him that even though you're believing Him to answer, that if for some reason He doesn't, you will continue to love, adore, respect, and serve Him because He is worthy!

Chapter Twelve
Ask God for Something Ridiculous and Expect a Spectacular Answer

"Now to Him who is able to do exceedingly abundantly above all that we ask or think, according to the power that works in us..."

Ephesians 3:20

The definition of ridiculous means absurd, preposterous, laughable. Think of the Scripture above. God is able to do infinitely more than anything you can ask or think. Think of something within the boundaries of His character and His expressed general will in the Bible. Something absurd, preposterous, or something so unlikely that it would cause folks to laugh at you if you shared it with them.

God is so mighty that if His power could be likened to all the sand in the world, answering your ridiculously unlikely prayer would require one millionth of a part of grain. Yes, chop that grain of sand into a million parts. One of those parts is all God needs. And, actually, because He's infinite, He can do it without even that part.

So why don't we see more mind-boggling prayers answered? Well, I think when we stand before God, we'll find that we saw many ridiculous prayers answered. Was anyone praying for the eradication of slavery in America? Was anyone praying for religious liberty in the Soviet Union before it fell so suddenly that the CIA flinched in surprise? Was anyone praying for a cure for polio before Jonas Salk stopped the paralyzing, deadly disease in its murderous tracks?

But that aside, the question is reasonable. After being in the company of the saints for over forty years, I think I'm on safe ground in saying if we aren't seeing answers to ridiculous prayers, it's because there are very few ridiculous prayers being prayed.

Our tendency is to pray safe. To pray in such generic terms, or in such a low-risk way that it's nearly impossible to determine whether the prayer is answered. But God is on the hunt for Christians who will give Him an opportunity to shock and awe the world by answering *ridiculous* prayers. "For the eyes of the Lord run to and from throughout the whole earth to show Himself strong on behalf of them whose heart is loyal toward Him" (1 Chronicles 16:9).

Pray Ridiculous Prayers!

Take a moment to think about your Christian faith. Everything about it is *ridiculous*. The miracles. The virgin birth. Heaven. Hell. The second coming of Christ. Everything. So asking you to pray ridiculous prayers is not asking you to do something extraordinary. Actually, though praying like this is rare, in a biblical sense, *it is ordinary*.

When I talk to a saint who has what appears to be an impossible situation, or one who desires something that seems impossibly out of reach, I counsel them to pray a ridiculous prayer. This means they must pray as though God has all power and is excitedly waiting for an opportunity to show what He can do despite everything that says it can't be done.

A ridiculous prayer puts all thoughts of limitations and lack on mute. It is careful to pray as though "with men this is impossible, but with God all things are possible" (Matthew 19:26).

A Personal Example of a Ridiculous Prayer

I was still in the military, and I was standing in the hall talking to someone. The person said something like, "It's a shame you'll have to retire without the possibility of making chief." What he was referring to was I was in a congressionally mandated military slot with a maximum possible pay grade of E-8. Pay grades for enlisted people are E-1 through E-9. I was E-8, which was great. But E-9, or Chief Master Sergeant, would have been fantastic! Unfortunately, *fantastic* was impossible.

I looked at the person and said, "That doesn't apply to me. If I want to make chief, I can pray and God will make a way for me even if He has to create a program just for me." I wasn't being arrogant. I was just speaking from a context of "with men this is impossible, but with God all things are possible."

Honestly, I don't recall actually praying for God to give me a chief slot. Nonetheless, a couple of months later a letter came down from national headquarters announcing the creation of a new program that opened the door for a person in the state to get promoted (I have a copy of the policy letter). The Lord did His God thing, and I was promoted to chief and retired as chief. Shortly thereafter, the program was rescinded. What a coincidence?

According to the Power that Works in Us

The Scripture we used in the opening refers to a door through which God's mighty power is released. That door is *us.* "According to the power that works in us." All the power in the world means nothing if it isn't released. The release comes either through God's sovereignty or our prayers, words, or actions. Our responsibility isn't God's sovereignty, it's praying and speaking and acting in a way that allows Him to be mighty in our behalf.

When told that I couldn't retire as chief, I could have looked at the policy and the fact that in the Georgia Air National Guard's fifty-five year history (at the time; 2003), no one in my job slot had ever been promoted to chief—and no one has since! Instead, my understanding of God's power and love for me caused me to instinctively defy that limitation. The ridiculously unlikely result of Him honoring my *ridiculous* statement of faith proves to me that He eagerly awaits opportunities to show Himself strong to those who will train themselves to see every mountain as a potential miracle.

Finally, I mentioned that I didn't actually pray for the chief's slot; I simply made a *ridiculous* declaration of faith. You see the same thing with the three Hebrew teens in Daniel 4 and Joshua and Caleb in Numbers 14. God honored their statements of faith as He would prayers of faith.

Lessons Learned

Lesson One. God takes pleasure in answering prayers that may be considered by some as ridiculous.

Lesson Two. I should train myself to see and speak as though mountains are possible miracles.

Prayer Exercise

1. Review your list. Is there something that you didn't put on there because the thought of God doing this for you is...well, ridiculous? Put it on the list!

2. Start doing the things we've talked about in the other chapters.

3. Open your eyes and ears. Ridiculous prayer answers may require you to take some action. The walls of Jericho miraculously coming down required something from the children of Israel (Joshua 6).

4. Look for those natural, practical things God may hav‍ you do to facilitate the answer. *Caution*: I'm not talkin‍ about helping God the way Sarah tried to help Hi‍ with Abraham's promise (Genesis 16). She caused‍ mess. I'm talking about acting in faith that it w‍ happen, not in fear that it won't.

Chapter Thirteen
Approach the Throne of Grace Boldly

*"For we do not have a High Priest
who cannot sympathize with our
weaknesses, but was in all points
tempted as we are, yet without sin.
Let us therefore come boldly to the
throne of grace, that we may
obtain mercy and find grace to
help in time of need."*

Hebrews 4:15, 16

Self-righteousness is a car without an engine; self-condemnation is a car without wheels. Although self-righteousness is the more worthless of the two vehicles, neither will get you one inch closer to answered prayer. We must repent for the sin of trusting in our own righteousness to approach God. We must repent for the sin of focusing so much on our weakness that we fail to trust in God's strength.

Mountains are formidable opponents. They are absolutely overwhelming. I've shared only a couple of my own prayer battles against mountains. So much is lost when the stories are put to paper. I come out of this looking so mighty and grand and unruffled. Never fear, the great man of faith is here!

That—is—absolutely—not—the—case!

Please, please, please, let your imagination run free as you ponder the misery that a mountain is able to inflict on a person who is trying with everything in him to believe biblical promises that seem like a fairy tale. My own prayer battles against mountains have been beyond excruciating. It's a combination of what happens if the mountain isn't moved, the time and regularity required to deal with the mountain, the loud, taunting mouth of the mountain, the unbelieving scrutiny of others as I deal with the mountain, the question of my own sinfulness as I battle the mountain, and the fact that God apparently doesn't own a watch or calendar!

Dealing with Self-Condemnation
While You Deal with a Mountain

Mountains are experts at getting us to focus on every real or imaginary reason why God shouldn't answer our prayers. They can be so overwhelming and energy-zapping that we simply don't have an ounce to spare wondering whether or not we're in good enough with God to get an audience, especially if the mountain has an approaching deadline that will further complicate things! So it's critical that we understand that the foundation of our success in prayer is built upon the success of our High Priest, Jesus Christ, and not whether we are good enough to have our prayers answered.

It's easy, even with short books like this one, to so complicate our approach to God that we get so tangled in the weeds of perfection that we forget that we're not dealing with a system or computer or sadistic professor. We're dealing with a kind, gracious, longsuffering, loving God—*who happens to be our Father!*

Think on these Scriptures for a minute or two. "For when we were still without strength, in due time Christ died for the ungodly...God demonstrates His love toward us, in that while we were still sinners, Christ died for us" (Romans 5:6, 8). How should truths like these affect our prayers?

My conclusion: There is no place for self-condemnation or *unhealthy* self-examination when we pray. We simply don't have time for it, especially when dealing with a mountain. *Come on, if God is that loving and patient to His enemies, is He going to be less loving and patient to His own children?* Read Hebrews 4:15, 16 again. We can boldly approach the throne room of God in prayer because of what Jesus accomplished in His life, death, and resurrection.

The Difference in the Conviction of the Holy Spirit, Self-Condemnation, and Unhealthy Self-Examination

Obviously, God has a claim on our lives. He is holy, and He demands that we be holy. This includes, but involves more than simply, being credited with the holiness of Christ. It means that as a lifestyle we yield to the voice of the Holy Spirit and the nature of the new creation that we have become through our adoption into God's family. Lifestyle obedience is a sign that we belong to God (1 John 3).

Yet, genuine children of God are capable of sin. In God's sovereignty and wisdom, He examines our lives as we pray and holds us accountable for growth and behavior. If He determines something amiss that requires immediate attention, the Holy Spirit convicts us to take action. An example is Jesus saying that we must first make good faith efforts to be reconciled with people who are offended with us before we pray. Or if the sin is in us, as in Mark 11:25, 26, we must repent before we proceed further in prayer.

This is good stuff. It leads to life and confidence in prayer.

Self-condemnation, on the other hand, mocks this whole process. It takes Scriptures like 1 John 1:9 and throws them out onto the street. "If we confess our sins, He is faithful and just to forgive us our sins and to cleanse us from all unrighteousness." What does it leave you with? Negative and doubt-filled feelings. *I can't be forgiven because I don't feel forgiven.*

And what leads to this toxic dump at the end of this dead-end street? Unhealthy self-examination. This is unlike the healthy self-examination of 2 Corinthians 13:5 that tells us to "examine yourselves as to whether you are in the faith." It's instead an unsanctified self-examination that sees our bad whether real or imaginary, but fails to see that the blood of Christ washes us clean of every sin repented of.

Rebuke the Mountain in the Righteousness of Christ

Don't bounce back and forth about your righteousness when you stand before a mountain. It'll only lead to a million reasons why God shouldn't answer your prayer. Instead, despite how you feel, stand on Scriptures like this one and believe what it says about you. "For He made Him [Jesus] who knew no sin to be sin for us, that we [this means *you*] might become the righteousness of God in Him" (2 Corinthians 5:20). Now, forget about *your* righteousness and boldly approach the throne of God in Jesus's righteousness.

Lessons Learned

Lesson One. Self-righteousness and self-condemnation will sabotage my prayers.

Lesson Two. If I repent of sin, I am forgiven by God whether I *feel* forgiven or not.

Lesson Three. I can boldly approach the throne of grace because I am righteous *in Christ*.

Practical Exercise

1. Confess out loud to yourself that you are righteous in Christ, and that you approach the throne room of God in the boldness of what Christ has accomplished for you.

2. Tell the Lord that no matter how inadequate you feel, you believe in the power of the blood of Jesus Christ that cleanses you from all sin.

3. Declare out loud to yourself that you enter boldly into the presence of the Lord.

Chapter Fourteen
It Is Your Father's Good Pleasure to Give You the Kingdom

*"Do not fear, little flock, for it is
your Father's good pleasure
to give you the kingdom."*

Luke 12:32

I'm filled with excitement at the prospect of multitudes of God's sons and daughters learning how to intelligently pray for spectacular answers. I *know* from Scriptural proof and from *personal* experience that as you put these truths to work, God is going to absolutely amaze you with His power, influence, and creativity. Indeed, after your first big prayer breakthrough, it's going to be hard for you not to pray what others may consider *ridiculous* prayers.

Yet there is one last truth I want to leave with you. It is the most important truth in this book. The one that makes all the others possible. It is this: *God gets great pleasure in lavishing spiritual and natural blessings on you.*

Beloved of God, the Bible opens in Genesis with God's children in paradise; it ends in Revelation with God's children in paradise. No one knows why this is, it just...*is.* For some inexplicable reason, God has an insatiable craving to spend eternity overwhelming us with endless revelations and expressions of His love for us (Ephesians 2:4-8). We are the objects of God's great love!

Use the methods I shared in this book? Yes, yes, please do. I know what they've done for me and others. But underlying any success you get in prayer using these methods or others is the fact that God wants to bless you more than you can imagine. As you pray, rest in His love and remind yourself constantly that "it is the Father's good pleasure to give unto [*me*] the kingdom."

Lesson Learned

Lesson. God wants to bless me more than I can imagine.

Practical Exercise

Before, during, and after you pray for something on your list, lift your hands to the Lord and pray, "Father, I thank You that it gives You great pleasure to do wonderful things for me. I don't understand why, but I won't fight you over it. I receive your goodness and kindness and mercy. I'm trying my best to learn as much as I can about prayer so that I can have a more effective prayer life. But I recognize that the greatest thing I can do to have a better prayer life is to have faith in your great kindness and to think often of how much you love me.

Testimonies

I would love to hear about your prayer breakthroughs. Please send your testimonies to the email address on the following page. You may also contact me with questions or comments. I do ask, however, that if you have comments that are appropriate for review purposes that you kindly post them on Amazon. They help a lot!

Prayer for Salvation

Absolutely, the most powerful prayer you can pray is for salvation. If God has brought you to a place of recognizing you have sinned against Him, and that you are a sinner who deserves His just eternal punishment, you can escape His judgment by repenting of your sins and believing the gospel. If you want out of your life of sin, and you want to live for God now, pray the prayer below.

God, be merciful to me, a sinner. I offer no excuses for my sins. I know that I can't save myself by simply reforming my behavior. I need to be made new in my spirit and soul and only You can do that. I believe that Jesus Christ is God in the flesh, and He has come to earth bodily to die for my sins.

I believe Jesus lived a sinless life for me. Jesus died on the cross for me. Jesus rose from the dead for me. And by faith I believe that as I ask God now for salvation, I am washed clean from my sins and their eternal consequences.

Thank You, Lord for saving me!

Please Leave A Review

Let's Stay In Touch!

Join my newsletter at www.ericmhill.com/newsletter. Here's
my contact info: facebook.com/ericmhillauthor or
ericmhillauthor@yahoo.com
or Twitter.com/ericmhillatl.

Other Books by Author

Spiritual Warfare Fiction
The Fire Series
Book 1: Bones of Fire
Book 2: Trial by Fire
Book 3: Saints on Fire

The Demon Strongholds Series
Book 1: The Spirit of Fear
Book 2: The Spirit of Rejection
Book 3: The Spirit of Ugly

Nonfiction
Deliverance from Demons and Diseases
What Preachers Never Tell You About Tithes & Offerings
Mistakes We Make When Casting Out Demons

God bless you!

Made in the USA
Las Vegas, NV
13 February 2024